FRONTIER DIARY

Macmillan McGraw-Hill

New York   Farmington

February 15, 1839

Rachel Stewart. That is my name, and today I am eight years old. I am writing this in the diary that was a birthday present from my family. It's strange to look through and see nothing but blank pages. I wonder what I will be writing on those pages. I know that one thing will be the story of a long trip. We are leaving our home here in Tennessee.

me

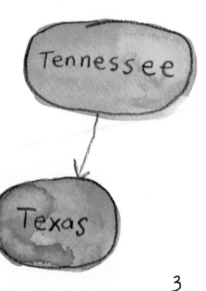

Tonight Ma and Pa told me and my brother Michael that we are going to Texas. Texas is a new country, almost a thousand miles south of Tennessee. Ma says there are lots of Americans living here. The land in Texas is very cheap. We will be able to have our own farm.

Tennessee

Texas

February 18, 1839

Michael doesn't want to go to Texas.
He is ten years old, and he wants to
stay here with his friend, Sam.
I didn't say so, but I will
miss our friends here, too.

Pa tried to cheer Michael up by
telling us about Texas. It used to be part of
Mexico, but the Texans didn't like that.
There was a fight at a place called the Alamo.
The Texans fought a much larger number of
Mexican soldiers. All the Texans at the
Alamo were killed. But that battle made the
rest of the Texans angry. So they fought
some more, and won their freedom.
One of the Texans who died at the Alamo
used to live here in Tennessee.
He was Congressman Davy Crockett.

March 1, 1839

We saw our neighbors for the last time today. They came to help us pack our wagon. We told them they could come back tomorrow and take any of our furniture that they need. We can't take it with us in the wagon. Abigail, my best friend, will get my bed. She always has had to share a bed with her sister. It seems funny to think of Abigail sleeping all alone in my bed. She was sad when she was here. She said she always wanted her own bed, but she didn't want me to leave.

March 2, 1839

We left before the sun came up this morning. But Sam was over to wave good-by. He gave Michael a rock as a present. Later I told Michael that was a funny present. But he said it was special because it was a Tennessee rock. In case they don't have rocks in Texas. I told him that was silly. But I wish we could take some of the beautiful Tennessee trees with us, too.

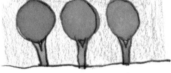

We sold our house to buy the mules that pull our wagon. I would rather have horses, but Pa says that mules are stronger.

The wagon is just like having a home that moves. We have everything we need in the wagon–even some corn seed to plant in Texas. That's some more of Tennessee we're taking with us.

At sundown, we stopped for the night.

6

March 3, 1839

I'm almost too tired to write. We're all
very tired every night. Yet all we do is sit
in the wagon all day. Ma and Pa sit up in
front. Michael and I are in the back. It's
crowded with food and clothes and even farm
tools and a saddle. I asked Pa why we couldn't
buy all these things when we get to Texas.
And why bring so much flour and salt and sugar?
We should have brought our furniture, I said.

Well, Pa explained that all these things will
cost much more in Texas. Texas is so far
away from where they make things like tools.
He said we can always make more furniture.
There's plenty of wood out there. But we're
bringing some nails. He said it's worth our
while to carry extra things to trade with, too.

Pa ———>

sugar

7

March 4, 1839

We've already traded some of our things, just like Pa said. Here's what happened.

Michael decided to run alongside the wagon. The mules move faster than I thought, but Michael kept up. He even ran ahead of us. Then he came tearing back. He had seen a couple of Indians standing by the road. I don't know why Michael was scared. He's seen Indians before. Anyway, we stopped when we came up to them. I climbed up on the seat next to Ma and saw them real close. They looked just like some trappers we've seen. In fact, they had some squirrels they'd killed.

Pa talked with the Indians in sign language. He traded some flour and sugar for six of their squirrels. We cooked them over a fire. They tasted a little like rabbit.

March 8, 1839

We're finished with the wagon for a while. We got to Memphis and found a boat that is going to New Orleans. We put our wagon and mules on board. The Mississippi is the biggest river I've ever seen. Ma says it gets to be more than a mile across farther down.

The river is flowing fast, now, because the spring thaw has begun up north. That should make our trip to New Orleans a quick one. I hope so. It isn't very nice on the boat. Tickets to ride up on top cost too much. So we have to stay below where there are lots of people and even livestock. It smells pretty bad. Michael thought he'd sneak up on top to see what it looked like, but they caught him right away. Nobody wears these old farm clothes up on top.

March 21, 1839

Not much to say about that awful trip downriver. We never got to see any of the country along the way. It rained almost the whole time, and there wasn't even a window. Anyway, we were below the water level.

We unloaded our wagon and the mules and spent this morning finding another boat. Just what I don't want! Another boat trip. This time we're going across the Gulf of Mexico to Galveston. Then we'll finally be in Texas!

I must say that the second boat looks better than the one we came downriver in. For one thing, the new boat is a sailing ship. And there aren't as many people going along.

But we'll have to wait here in New Orleans a few days. We're staying in an old boarding house now.

March 23, 1839

We've made some new friends—the Martin family.
They are staying in this boarding house, too.
Mr. and Mrs. Martin are about the same age
as Ma and Pa. They have four children.
There is Tyrone, who is twelve, and Hannah,
who is my age. And there is Amy, who is five.
They have a baby, too. The Martins have come
from Ohio. They are going to the same place
we are—Texas. But the Martins have been
waiting here two months. They lost most of
their belongings in a boat accident. Their
relatives in Ohio are sending more things
to them. Mr. Martin and Tyrone unload boats
to earn money. They say they soon
will have enough to replace
what was lost.
I feel sorry for them.
Mr. and Mrs. Martin
always look worried.

March 24, 1839

Today we spent all day walking around
New Orleans. Memphis and Scottsville
back home are nothing like this. New Orleans
is much larger. And there are so many
more people. But they are all dressed
so funny. They look like they're going
to a party in the middle of the day !
I saw a black man wearing a blue velvet
suit finer than any I ever saw. I asked
Pa why a slave would dress up like that.
He said there are lots of black men
here who aren't slaves. In fact, some of
them are shipowners and rich merchants.

The people speak different languages
here, too. Ma says some speak
Spanish and some speak French,
and some people speak both.
I don't know how the people here
can keep things straight.

<u>March 26, 1839</u>

I almost got in trouble today. I called Tyrone Martin a liar. Was he angry! Here is what he said.

Back one night in February, the Martins heard a lot of noise outside. They went out to see what all the fuss was. It was a holiday they have called "Mardi Gras." Tyrone said there were people marching through the city carrying torches. And everybody was dressed up in strange costumes. Most of them wore masks, too.

He said they looked like kings and queens and big animals. Some of them rode on horse-pulled carts as big as river barges.

Well, that's as far as he got before I said he was making it up. But his sister, Hannah, told me it was all true. I hope he doesn't stay mad at me.

April 3, 1839

We left New Orleans early this morning. This boat is much different from the one that took us down the Mississippi. The captain is a nice man. He lets us come up on deck and see where we are going. All you can see is water, but the waves and sky are beautiful.

Captain

The city of Galveston is where we are headed. Ma showed us on a map how we are going.

This huge ship has 60 people and their wagons and horses on board. But the wind is pulling it along. The sails of this ship look as hard as rocks when you see them stretched tight by the wind. But when the sailors draw them up, you can see that they are just pieces of strong cloth.

April 10, 1839

I must say, I liked New Orleans better
than Galveston. But Michael loves it.
The streets are filled with rough-looking men
on horses. The men all wear animal skins
for clothes. They aren't anything like the
fine gentlemen of New Orleans. The streets
here are nothing but dirt paths. The mud
is thick and deep. It would swallow you up
if you fell in it.

I feel lonely because there is no one my age
to talk with. The Martins stayed in New Orleans.
They said they would see us in Texas someday.
I wonder if they will.

Well, Michael just told me something.
He found out that this place used to be
the headquarters of Jean Lafitte,
the pirate.

April 14, 1839

We left the pirate's den and are on our way
again. I never thought I'd be so glad to see
those two mules pull our wagon. Even the mules
looked happy to be leaving Galveston !

Here is our plan. Pa found out from a man
in Galveston that good land is being sold
near San Antonio. That is about 200 miles
from here. We can be there in less than
a month if we have good weather. That way,
we can get a corn crop in by the middle
of June. Pa says we'll need the corn
to trade with during the winter.

Texas looks very different from Tennessee.
There aren't nearly as many trees.
I remember how hard Pa had to work back home
clearing the land to plant. Here you can
just push the seeds in the ground and
get out of the way.

April 16, 1839

We met a Texas family yesterday. Their name
is Meyenberg. They asked us to have supper
and stay the night. I take back everything I said
in Galveston about Texans. The Meyenbergs
are as nice as anybody we knew in Tennessee.

The Meyenbergs came here from Germany
only a few years ago. We had a wonderful meal,
fixed German-style. All the food, even the
meat, came from Mr. Meyenberg's farm.
Mr. Meyenberg told us that anybody who
works hard can do well here in Texas.

Afterwards, I got to sleep in a clean, fresh bed.
As I fell asleep, I thought how nice
it will be to have our own house again.

April 18, 1839

We've moved slowly the last two days. We have been traveling through swampy land. The wheels of the wagon sink into the ground and get caught. And the mosquitoes are just terrible.

The mosquitoes were so bad tonight that we could hardly eat supper. We ate fish that we traded some salt to an Indian for. The Indian had lots of fish. He was shooting them in the water with a bow and arrow.

The Indian was smeared all over with some kind of grease. He told Pa that the grease kept mosquitoes from biting him.

I thought that grease smelled awful then, but I wish we had some now.

May 4, 1839

Finally we are in San Antonio. It is a busy city, but nicer than Galveston. There are a lot of people here who speak Spanish, so it seems a little like New Orleans.

We saw the Alamo. It is right in the center of town. It used to be a church. Michael and I went inside. They left it just the way it was when the Mexicans captured it. It was quiet and kind of creepy.

Everyone here is very proud of Texas. Pa went to meet a man about buying some land. While he was gone, we talked to a woman who said she had known Davy Crockett. She was from Tennessee, too. She said that people talked about Texas becoming part of the United States. But she thought the United States should become part of Texas.

May 15, 1839

Today we are home. We are on our own land.
It is about 15 miles from San Antonio.
The land is beautiful grassland. It has a
few trees and a lot of little bushes.

Tonight we will sleep in the wagon, but tomorrow
we will start working on our new house.
We will build it right by the two biggest
oak trees. They will shade the house and
protect it from the wind.

After we have a place to live, we will plant
the corn. We can get a crop in time for
the winter. After we plant the seeds, it will take
about three months to harvest. That is,
if the rain doesn't wash it away, or the dry
weather burn it up. I wonder what would
happen to us then. We have spent
most of our money.

May 18, 1839

Our house is going up. There is a sawmill
between here and town. We got wood
for the house there. In return, they can cut down
some of our oak trees. Oak is very hard wood.
This makes it harder to build with,
but the house will last a very long time.

Michael and I are working, too. We are clearing
the land where we will plant corn. I was wrong
when I thought it would be easy to plant crops.
There are a lot of hard, dry little bushes
growing here. They are called sagebrush.
Pulling them out of the ground makes
your back tired.

Still, I'd rather be here than in that wagon
all day. It was nice to see so much of
the country. But now we have our own place,
and it will always be our home.

21

June 1, 1839

Today is Michael's birthday. He is
eleven. We gave him a knife we bought
back in San Antonio. It was the kind
they call a Bowie knife. It was named
after Colonel James Bowie, the leader
of the Texans who fought at the Alamo.
Colonel Bowie invented the shape
of this knife blade. Michael heard
about Colonel Bowie while we were in
San Antonio. He was very happy
with the knife. He went right out and
cut down some sagebrush with it.

We had our first real meal in the house
for Michael's birthday. A Mexican man
brought us a table that he had made.
Pa traded him some sugar for it.
The man lives near here.
He has some children our same ages.

June 10, 1839

Pa had to go into town today. He took Ma and
Michael and me as far as the Hernandez farm.
They are our Mexican neighbors. Mr. Hernandez
is really more of a carpenter than a farmer.
His sons and his brother and his nephews
take care of the farm. Mr. Hernandez is a
good carpenter, and people come from
all around to get him to make things.
Pa met him at the sawmill.

Maria Hernandez is the youngest in the family.
She is eight. She is going to teach us how to
speak Spanish. The Hernandez family
came from Mexico a long time ago. They are
proud to be Texans. Some of
Mr. Hernandez' sons fought for Texas
in the war. They have a big Texas flag
flying in front of their house.

23

June 15, 1839

Michael could have left that
Tennessee rock at home. We found out
today there are plenty of rocks in Texas.
We began plowing the land to plant our corn.
Every time the plow hit a rock, Michael and I
had to pull it out. We made two big piles
of rocks on each side of the field.
And we're not even finished.

Now I see why Pa wanted to bring along
mules instead of horses. Those two mules
may be slow, but they're stronger
than horses—especially when it comes
to hard work like pulling a plow.

Michael found an arrowhead
when we were picking out rocks.
It looks like a thin rock, but
you can see where it was chipped
into shape. Michael put it under
his bed with his Tennessee rock.

24

Arrowhead →

July 4, 1839

What a day this has been! They celebrate
Independence Day here just as they do
in the United States. Nobody is sure why.
I guess it's because there are so many
Americans living here. The people are
more excited here than at home.

There were many games and races.
Michael won a foot race, and the prize
was a silver coin.

A lot of important people made speeches.
They weren't very interesting.
We saw Sam Houston, though. He used
to be president of Texas. Before that,
he was governor of Tennessee. He said
Texas should be part of the United States.
All the people cheered at that. I did, too.

July 10, 1839

We're settled now. The house is finished,
except for paint and a few things.
We haven't got any windows or a fireplace
yet, but we won't need those till winter.

The corn has started to come up. We had
a good rain the other day. That helped a lot.

There are many animals here so we always
have meat. There are wild turkeys just like
the ones in Tennessee. Michael and I
caught one by walking up behind it and
hitting it with a stick. They are huge birds.
If you aren't careful, they can hurt you
with their beaks. It was quite a job
pulling out all the feathers. But it was
a big bird, and we had meat for a week.

August 16, 1839

Crops are starting to come in now.
Not ours, though. We got a late start.
But the corn at the Hernandez farm
is ready. Michael and I went over
to help them harvest the first crop.
When it's ready to pick, it has to be
picked quickly.

The Hernandez family has a big ox
and a cart to carry the corn. That ox
is the biggest animal I ever saw.
He's stronger than both our mules
put together. But he lets even
Michael lead him around like a puppy.

I was tired from working all day, but
no one went to bed early. Maria's cousins
brought their guitars, and we sang
and danced till late.

September 20, 1839

Hooray! Our friends, the Martins, arrived from New Orleans today. Pa said we had room for them until they got a start on their own place in the spring.

Fresh milk

They brought some cows with them. It will be nice to have fresh milk again. Pa and Mr. Martin are talking about raising more cows.

Tyrone is going to help Pa and Mr. Martin finish up our fireplace and chimney. Next week we'll use Mr. Hernandez' ox cart to bring the glass for the windows up from San Antonio. Then we'll have a <u>real</u> home.

Michael loves having Tyrone here. And Hannah and Amy will sleep with me. It's fun having a full house.

October 18, 1839

Maria Hernandez was here to help pick
our corn crop. We don't have as much corn
as they did, but it will see us through the winter.
While we were picking corn, a strong wind
came up. We could feel the weather turn cold
all of a sudden. It got so cold we had to
get coats. Maria told us this sudden cold
happens a lot here. They call it a "norther."
Soon it will be winter. The corn is ripe
just in time.

We are drying and salting meat
for the winter. We hang it up
in long strips. When it is dry,
we store it in the attic of
the house. The attic looks like
a store. It smells very good.

December 25, 1839

Our first Christmas in Texas.
We visited the Hernandez family.
At their house, we were given
"piñatas." A "piñata" is a bag
that hangs from the ceiling.
They blindfold you, and you take a stick
and try to break the "piñata."
Inside Michael's "piñata" was a
belt buckle. I had a beautiful
scarf inside mine.

We had a wonderful Christmas dinner.
And then we rode into San Antonio.
There people set off fireworks
in the main square. Everything was
very exciting, but I'm almost
too tired to write about it.

February 14, 1840

The end of a wonderful year. And the last page
in this book. We have a warm house
and lots of new friends. There is plenty of food.
But a lot of work to do, too. We have clothes
to make. And Michael has the job of milking
the cows. Tyrone brings us firewood.
Those oak logs burn a long time.

I have something else to do, too.
I was surprised to find that Hannah and Amy Martin
cannot read. So, I am teaching them some
every day now. Tyrone listens in, too.
I think he is too proud to say he wants to learn.

I know one thing. I will save this diary.
It will be a record of our family. Perhaps
my children will want to read it someday.